THIS PAMPHLET IS TO BE
INCLUDED IN THE EMERGENCY
PACKS OF AIRCRAFT OPERATING
OVER THE ARCTIC

ARCTIC

SURVIVAL

A.M. PAMPHLET 226

PENGUIN BOOKS

PENGUIN BOOKS

UK | USA | Canada | Ireland | Australia
India | New Zealand | South Africa

Penguin Books is part of the Penguin Random House group of companies
whose addresses can be found at global.penguinrandomhouse.com.

First published by the Air Ministry 1953
First published in Penguin Books 2017
002

The moral right of the author has been asserted

Printed in Great Britain by Clays Ltd, Elcograf S.p.A.

A CIP catalogue record for this book is available from the British Library

ISBN: 978–1–405–93168–7

www.greenpenguin.co.uk

ARCTIC

SURVIVAL

ARCTIC SURVIVAL

INTRODUCTION

1. Survival depends on two, largely psychological, factors: the determination to live and the elimination of fear. Fear is caused through ignorance, in other words *inadequate training*. However, no amount of training or other material aid will suffice without the natural instinct of self-preservation.

2. **The Arctic.** The Arctic has been defined geographically as the area north of the Arctic Circle at latitude 66°33′N. From the survival aspect, however, it is more practical to consider the area north of the timber line as Arctic. Along certain Siberian rivers forests grow up to 400 miles north of the Arctic Circle, while along the west shore of the Hudson Bay the tree line is 400 miles south of the Circle. These areas north of the timber line, with a mean annual temperature below 32°F., are known as "barren lands". The region includes the north coasts of Alaska, Canada, Scandinavia, and the U.S.S.R.; the Canadian Arctic Archipelago, Greenland, and the majority of Iceland.

3. **The Sub-Arctic.** The sub-arctic is a belt of coniferous vegetation of variable width south of the Arctic Circle. Within it the mean annual temperature is above 32°F. It includes most of Alaska and the interior of Canada, the northern territories of the U.S.S.R., and most of Scandinavia. The term must be used flexibly.

4. **Other Cold Regions.** The principles of arctic survival have to be applied to other mountainous or desolate regions where low temperatures at high altitudes, high winds, a permanent snow covering, or other wintry phenomena prevail at various times. These regions include the Rocky Mountains, the Andes, and the Himalayas.

5. **The Arctic Climate.** The Arctic is bleak, and in the winter cold, but it is not, as many people think, a region of continual snowstorms and howling gales where the temperature is always "sixty below". Many Eskimos and quite a few white people live

3

there contentedly. The idea that snow is always falling arises from the fact that snow is easily stirred by the wind long after it has stopped falling. The two seasons, a long winter and a short summer, are clearly defined and the temperature varies considerably. In general, the interior areas have the coldest winters and the warmest summers. A temperature of —96°F. has been recorded in Central Siberia. At the other end of the scale, temperatures of 80°F. in the shade are common in many places north of the Arctic Circle. The annual temperature range may be as much as 176°F.; as at Fort Yukon, on the Arctic Circle, where a maximum summer temperature of 100°F. in the shade, and a minimum winter temperature of —76°F., have been recorded. With these high temperatures it is not unusual to find a summer landscape which can be favourably compared with the Orkneys and Shetlands.

PRE-FLIGHT PREPARATION

Prepare for Trouble

6. The best time to start learning what to do when you have been forced down in arctic regions is before the event. The correct preparation involves acquiring a thorough knowledge of:—

    (a) Cold-weather flying clothing.

    (b) Safety and survival equipment.

    (c) Emergency drills and procedures.

    (d) The principles of survival.

Cold-Weather Flying Clothing

7. Cold-weather flying clothing has been designed to enable aircrew to fly effectively in any types of aircraft, and particular emphasis has been made on freedom of movement. The main essentials are to keep windproof outer materials intact over sufficient inner insulative clothing, and the avoidance of any tight or restrictive clothing. In survival conditions you must depend for warmth, not on fires or fuel stoves, but on your clothing. Your clothing is your first line of defence against low temperatures and high winds. BE PREPARED. Dress for the possible emergency and adjust the temperature of the cockpit accordingly.

8. Inner Clothing. The principle of correct underclothing is not thickness but insulation. Air in fact forms the main insulation of all materials used in clothing. The inner flying clothing consists of multiple layers of loosely fitting garments each designed to fit over the clothing immediately beneath it, holding a layer of air between the garments. Your inner clothing will normally consist of:—

    (*a*) A string vest made of thick cotton cord, knitted in a wide mesh. The wide mesh holds a layer of air in contact with the body.

Fig. 1.
Cold Weather Flying Clothing

    (*b*) Pyjama-type inner trousers worn under war service or flying dress trousers. The looseness of the underpants holds air and allows free circulation and ventilation. In very cold conditions two pairs should be worn.

    (*c*) A woollen aircrew shirt with attached collar and buttoning cuffs. A tie should not be worn during flight because it would restrict ventilation at the neck.

    (*d*) A long-sleeved, slit-necked, ribbed woollen pollover. A draw cord is provided at the neck opening to help in the control of ventilation.

    (*e*) A necksquare made of soft cotton and resembling a large dishcloth. It effectively protects the neck opening and allows some ventilation at the neck. It is designed to protect the face in high wind conditions, and at night when the face is the only part of the body not protected by the sleeping bag.

5

9. **Outer Clothing.** Outer garments must be windproof and durable. The weave must be close to prevent snow compacting into the material. A certain degree of porosity is necessary to allow water vapour to escape and evaporate in the cold dry air. You will normally wear:—

(a) A cold-weather flying overall which is essentially two garments, trousers and jacket, which have been combined to make an overall as this is more effective in flight conditions. For ground survival the jacket, or inner parka, and the trousers can be separated to allow adequate ventilation. Draw cords are provided at the bottoms of the trousers legs: these are intended for use in survival conditions to help in keeping snow out of the trousers and boot tops. A hood is attached to the jacket and in normal flying conditions it is folded neatly at the back. The face aperture can be closed by a draw cord.

(b) A cold-weather cap made of windproof material and lined with woollen fabric. It may be worn alone or under the hood of the flying overall or outer parka. The cap has internally stowed flaps which can be turned down to give protection to the back of the neck, ears, and forehead.

(c) An outer parka to be worn in extreme cold over the flying overall. It has both windproof and insulating properties. The collar, to which the hood is attached, is fur-lined. The hood, closed by a draw cord, is designed to protect the face in high wind chill conditions. An extension to the hood, for use in the severest weather, consists of an adjustable wire-stiffened curtain edged with wolverine fur, and helps in preventing the wind reaching the face.

10. **Handwear.** Handwear must be insulating and windproof, and must not be tight. Mittens are preferred to gloves as the fingers will give mutual warmth, but mittens are not ideal for air-crew. The handwear assembly consists of:—

(a) Long woollen wristlets which give protection to the wrist and the back of the hand.

(b) Inner mitts made of wool.

(*c*) Outer mitts made of soft leather. The palm of the hand is lined with a wool pile material, and a pad of the same material is sewn on the back. This pad is used for warming the nose or the face in the event of frostbite, and also as a nose wiper.

(*d*) Working gloves, made with leather fronts and fabric backs, to be worn over the wristlets.

11. **Footwear.**

(*a*) *The Mukluk Assembly* is worn instead of flying boots by aircrew operating in dry cold conditions. It consists of:—

(i) Three pairs of woollen socks sized to fit over one another without creasing.

(ii) A duffle sock made of blanketing and sized to fit effectively over the woollen socks.

(iii) A thick felt insole, with a ventilating mesh sole, worn downwards, to provide effective insulation beneath the foot.

(iv) A mukluk which has a waterproof canvas upper extending over the calf and a rubber sole and galosh. The sole is ribbed for good traction on snow. The top of the boot can be closed by a draw cord.

(*b*) *The Boucheron* is worn by personnel operating in wet cold conditions. This boot has a leather waterproof upper extending to just below the knee, and a rubber sole and galosh. It is unlined but has a removable felt insole. It may be worn over the woollen socks and duffle sock as required.

Safety and Survival Equipment

12. Before each flight carefully check all aircraft emergency packs and your personal survival kit and safety equipment. Equipment on personal loan should be inspected daily. Ensure that all the articles in your personal survival pack are serviceable and that none is missing. Resist the temptation to "borrow" desirable items for your personal use. Make yourself thoroughly familiar with the operation of your safety equipment. Do not misuse it; rough handling may lead to failure at a critical time. Since weight and bulk are the limiting factors in the amount of survival equipment that can be carried in an aircraft, your parachute,

lifejacket, and dinghy, are regarded as supplementary survival equipment. Study your safety equipment from this angle; look upon your parachute as potential shelter, clothing, or fishing equipment. Likewise, each item in your survival packs has been selected and designed to have as many uses as possible. Learn them all NOW.

Emergency Drills and Procedures

13. It is not within the scope of this pamphlet to discuss emergency drills and procedures in detail. A.M. Pamphlet 212, "Emergencies", and the Command Emergency Drills deal fully with these subjects. Emergency drills should be practised regularly, so that the drill will be almost automatic even in total darkness, and you should thoroughly know the emergency signals procedure and the rescue facilities available in the area over which you intend to fly.

Principles of Survival

14. If you wish to survive an emergency descent into the Arctic, there are certain things you must do. This pamphlet tells you what to do and in many cases how to do it. A copy of the pamphlet will be inside your survival pack. Read it for the first time in the comfort of a crew-room, not on an ice floe drifting in the Arctic Sea.

ACTION IN AN EMERGENCY

Communication

15. The provision of effective help to aircraft and personnel in distress depends, to a large extent, on the receipt of timely and accurate information by the ground organization. When the captain of an aicraft considers that a state of "Safety", "Urgency", or "Distress", exists, the appropriate signals should be transmitted in accordance with the current procedures. Do not hesitate to let the world and your crew know that an emergency exists.

Abandon Aircraft or Crash-land?

16. If an emergency arises over the Arctic, land the aircraft if it is at all possible. Abandon the aircraft only if the terrain is

extremely hazardous or in the event of structural failure or fire in the air. Landing with the aircraft has the advantages of providing a readily distinguishable marker for search aircraft, and many parts of the aircraft will prove invaluable later on.

Abandoning Aircraft

17. If you do have to abandon the aircraft take as much equipment as possible with you. If you have followed the practice of wearing all your cold-weather flying clothing you will leave the aircraft with adequate protection against the cold. Note the position of the crashed aircraft; even a burnt-out wreck may be of some use. Large crews should decide, before the emergency arises, on a method of assembly after abandoning aircraft. Here are two suggested procedures:—

(*a*) Bail-out on a straight course. The crew can assemble progressively. The two end men, the first and last out, move inward toward the middle men, linking up with others on the way. The magnetic track of the aircraft should be given to all the crew before they bail-out. The middle man should light a fire and make smoke signals, and flash his heliograph to mark the rendezvous.

(*b*) Bail-out in a circle and all personnel converge toward the centre.

In both procedures the crew should bail-out in quick succession to ensure that they will not be too widely dispersed.

Crash Landing

18. When searching for a place to land, stay on track if it is at all possible. Do not wander aimlessly until all the fuel has gone; endeavour to make a crash landing under power. Successful forced landings have been made on frozen lakes or rivers, beaches, large ice floes, glaciers or ice-caps, and treeless valleys. Always land with your wheels UP.

19. If there is a choice do not land on frozen lakes or rivers during the thaw or freeze-up; the ice may be too thin. Do not land on sea ice which appears dark in colour, or on any ice free from snow drifts. You should normally land into wind: blowing snow will give you an indication of the wind direction. However, the

presence of pressure ridges, formed when ice floes grind into or ride up over each other, and tightly packed snow drifts, will necessitate a landing parallel to the ridges or drifts.

IMMEDIATE ACTIONS AFTER A CRASH LANDING

20. Get out of the aircraft as quickly as possible, taking with you your safety and survival equipment. Be cautious as to the state of the ground around the aircraft. Deep crevasses may exist in glaciated regions and avalanches may be prevalent on steep slopes. Stay away from the aircraft until the danger of fire has passed and then remove all useful items of equipment from the aircraft. The battery should be removed and kept as warm as possible. It is advisable to spread a parachute on the snow and place all the equipment on it to prevent loss. First aid for the injured is the next consideration. While first aid is being given, make certain that everyone is properly dressed. Special clothing, such as anti-G suits, which tend to restrict circulation, should be loosened or taken off.

21. **First Aid.** Check all the crew for injuries and shock. All injured personnel should be kept as warm as possible to prevent frostbite or freezing. Follow the established practices:—

(a) *Wounds.* See that open wounds are dressed to prevent infection; do not handle the wound and keep the wounded part at rest. Clothing should be cut away with care. Slit it carefully so that it can be sewn up again after the wound has been treated.

(b) *Fractures.* Fractured limbs should be immobilized by splints. Do not use metal parts of the aircraft for splints. Do not remove clothing from the limb, but cut it away from wounds and dress them before splinting.

(c) *Haemorrhage.* Bleeding will normally be stopped by the blood congealing in the very low temperature. If necessary apply a tourniquet between the injury and the heart, at the pressure point nearest to the injury. Release the tourniquet for a half-a-minute every fifteen to twenty minutes, and remove it entirely as soon as possible.

(*d*) **Shock and Internal Injury.** Keep the injured person lying down and warm. If he is conscious a hot drink can be given, provided the injury is not abdominal.

(*e*) **Burns.** Don't open blisters. Use the anti-burn cream in the first-aid kit. Don't change the bandage and keep the burned part at rest.

(*f*) **Cessation of Breathing.** If an injured man has stopped breathing, pull his tongue forward and apply artificial respiration. Check for head injuries or fractured skull, indicated by unequal pupils or bleeding from the ears or into the skin around the eyes.

22. **Drain the Oil.** If possible, oil should be drained from the engine sump and oil tank to provide an immediate source of fuel for heat and cooking. Failure to do so as soon as possible will result in the oil becoming congealed and impossible to drain. A receptacle is not vital, as the oil can be drained on to the ground where it will congeal quickly.

23. **Sundry Hints.** When the immediate tasks have been completed start a fire in a sheltered spot and sit down and relax. Firm handling of the situation is necessary from the start. The captain of the aircraft will assume command of the party, but if another member of the crew is better qualified he should always be consulted before any major decisions are made. The provision of shelter, warmth, and food, and the preparation of the emergency signalling equipment should be attended to next. Detail the crew members for camp duties according to their capabilities and fitness; but do not overwork the willing horse. For duties away from the immediate camp site men should work in pairs, so that they can watch each other's faces for the first signs of frostbite. Injured members of the party should be given small tasks to do, to occupy their minds and to overcome the feeling that they are a burden on the survivors. Such duties could include whittling wood for kindling, making fish nets, and log keeping. The log should tell the complete story from the beginning of the emergency to your safe return to civilization. All observations, however trivial they may seem at the time, should be recorded.

EMERGENCY SIGNALS

24. As soon as possible all your emergency signalling equipment should be prepared for use. Search aircraft have often flown

over or near the scene of a crash without seeing it. Survivors should take turns keeping watch for search aircraft and everyone should be familiar with the location and operation of the emergency signalling equipment. One of the best ground signals is the aircraft itself; and to achieve the maximum contrast against a background of snow, its surfaces should be kept clear of snow and frost. If your dinghy and weather apron are not required for anything more important, use them to make signal strips and compose a message from the Ground/Air Emergency Code. Make the kite of the "Gibson Girl" more conspicuous by attaching a long tail to it. The tail can be made from a parachute canopy and coloured with fluorescene sea marker. Make the camp site as conspicuous as possible from the air.

Fig. 2. Display of Ground Signals

Radio Signals

25. **Aircraft W/T.** The aircraft W/T is your best means of communication. If transmissions are made, the message, bearing an S.O.S. priority, should include the aircraft callsign, the estimated position, a 20-second dash, and the time at which you intend to transmit again. Transmissions on 500 Kcs. should start at 15 and 45 minutes past each hour, for periods of three minutes. In the low winter temperatures the batteries will be very weak, and transmissions should be made as soon as possible after the crash before the batteries freeze.

26. **The Standard Dinghy Radio Kit—SCR 578— "Gibson Girl".**

(*a*) The transmitter should be operated for periods of four minutes, at intervals of about ten minutes. But if a serviceable and accurate watch is available, you should transmit for periods of three minutes starting at 15 and 45 minutes past each hour.

(*b*) With the signals set to automatic, the signals take the following form:—

(i) Auto 1 Position—S.O.S. for 20 seconds followed by a continuous dash for 20 seconds.

(ii) Auto 2 Position—S.O.S. for 20 seconds followed by four-second dashes for 20 seconds.

As the Auto 2 Position is designed to operate the automatic alarm on surface vessels, transmissions in Arctic regions should be confined to the Auto 1 Position, unless it is estimated that the crash position is such that transmissions on the Auto 2 Position may be received by surface craft. In this case the four-minute period should consist of two minutes on the Auto 1 Position followed by two minutes on the Auto 2 Position.

(*c*) If the crash position is known, this can be transmitted along with any other information, on the Manual Position, outside the above periods.

(*d*) For convenience the transmitter may be strapped to a tree. If the wind is not strong enough to fly the kite, you may extend the aerial to its maximum length between trees: to earth the set, extend the spare reel of aerial wire parallel to and below the aerial and fasten the "ground" lead to this.

13

If there are no trees, extend the aerial to its maximum length along the ground: to earth the set, extend the spare reel of aerial wire along the surface of the ground in the opposite direction to the aerial, and fasten it to the "ground" lead.

27. **Transmitter T3180—"Walter".** With a maximum range of 20 to 25 miles, "Walter" should be used only when it is estimated that search aircraft are in the vicinity. It is pointless to switch on "Walter" immediately after the crash, unless the aircraft is on a recognized route frequented by other aircraft. The transmitter should be switched on for periods of two minutes at five-minute intervals, and should be left switched on if aircraft are seen or heard. In Arctic conditions the battery should be worn permanently under one's clothing and attached to the transmitter by a wandering lead.

Shadow Signals

28. One of the best shadow signals in winter is snow writing. Trenches cut in the snow to form a message are easy to make. They can be made simply by scuffling up snow as one walks along. The bigger the size of the letter and the deeper the shadow, the more effective is the signal. Normally, however, 30-foot letters are big enough. Shadows may be deepened by cutting the trenches and piling the snow where it will throw the longest shadow along the letters; that is, write your message facing north or south and pile the snow to the south of the letters. The writing or the geometrical design can be brought into sharper contrast with the snow by filling the trench with spruce boughs or parts of the aircraft, or by mixing the fluorescene sea marker with water and sprinkling it in the trench. In summer, writing can be made in the sand. On the tundra, sod blocks can be cut out and set aside to cast shadows on the bare earth. Logs or rocks can be laid out on any surface. In spring, snow drifts can often be found in willows, under high banks and in gullies, long after snow has gone from the flat country. It can be shovelled on to dark ground to form signals. When snow lays lightly on the tundra, dig down to expose the dark contrasting tundra. In the deep Arctic winter, a full or almost full moon will throw excellent shadows of well-prepared trench writing on snow surfaces. The best signals are either S.O.S. or ⊕. Qualifying signals should be taken from the Ground/Air Emergency Code. (Fig. 3.)

Ground/Air Emergency Code for Use In Air/Land Rescue Search

KEY

1 REQUIRE DOCTOR, SERIOUS INJURIES
2 REQUIRE MEDICAL SUPPLIES
3 UNABLE TO PROCEED
4 REQUIRE FOOD AND WATER
5 REQUIRE FIREARMS AND AMMUNITION
6 REQUIRE MAP AND COMPASS
7 REQUIRE SIGNAL LAMP WITH BATTERY, & RADIO
8 INDICATE DIRECTION TO PROCEED
9 AM PROCEEDING IN THIS DIRECTION
10 WILL ATTEMPT TAKE-OFF
11 AIRCRAFT SERIOUSLY DAMAGED
12 PROBABLY SAFE TO LAND HERE
13 REQUIRE FUEL AND OIL
14 ALL WELL
15 NO
16 YES
17 NOT UNDERSTOOD
18 REQUIRE ENGINEER

CODE

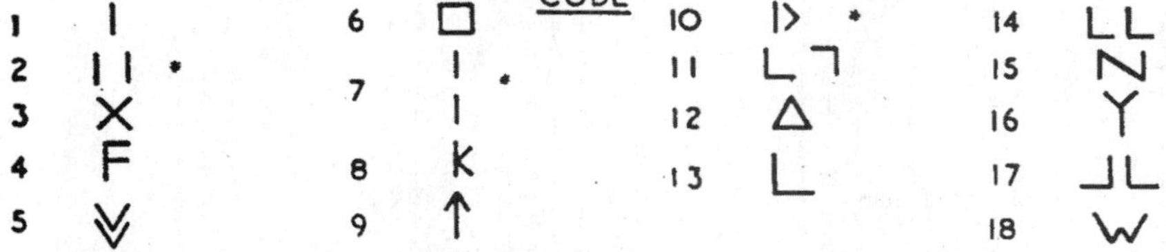

* A SPACE OF 10 FT BETWEEN ELEMENTS WHEREVER POSSIBLE

Fig. 3.

Fire and Smoke Signals

29. Smoke signals are satisfactory only on calm clear days. Winds and blowing snow tend to disperse the smoke, so that it is visible only at very short distances. Create a smoke which will be in contrast to the background; *i.e.* white smoke in summer and black in winter. White smoke can be made by throwing green grass and boughs on the fires, and black smoke by throwing on rubber or oil.

30. Signal fires should not be burned continuously if fuel is scarce. The fires should be prepared and covered to prevent the materials from getting wet or covered with snow. Three signal fires arranged in a triangle is a distress sign. If convenient, use the camp fire as one of the signal fires. Otherwise arrange the fires around the camp site, so that they can be reached and lit with a minimum of delay.

31. The spruce torch (*i.e.* a flaming spruce tree) is an excellent signal by day or night. Select a tree with very dense foliage, and shake off as much snow and ice as possible from the upper branches. If all the trees in the vicinity are sparse, break branches from other trees, shake them free of snow and weave them in the upper branches of the selected tree. Then collect kindling and build a "bird's nest" in the lower branches to act as the ignitor. If possible have a can of fuel or oil at hand to hasten the ignition. Cover the "bird's nest" for protection against the weather, and so that newly accumulated snow can be knocked off the tree without falling on to the kindling. The "bird's nest" will ignite the spruce tips until the whole tree is ablaze and visible for miles.

Light Signals

32. Use the heliograph for signalling if the sun is shining. Heliographs can be improvised from any polished surfaces, such as cowlings and ration tins. Signalling by these means should be practised regularly so that there is no delay in focusing when an aircraft is sighted.

33. At night your best light signals are the torch and the flash fire. The flash fire is made by soaking a large piece of fabric in high octane fuel, spreading it out on the ground and lighting it.

When using a signalling torch or the signalling lamp of the "Gibson Girl", do not point it in the direction of the search aircraft. Illuminate a reflective surface, such as an inverted cowling or any snow-covered surfaces, by pointing the beam downwards at a low angle so that a large lighted circle is reflected. Keep the light moving or flash S.O.S. to improve the chances of being seen.

Pyrotechnics

34. You will have a limited supply of emergency pyrotechnics, and possibly the aircraft signal pistol and cartridges. Fire them only when you are fairly certain that there is a chance of them being seen by the search aircraft. The search aircraft at night, using the Night Search Technique, will fire green cartridges every 5 to 10 minutes. When the survivors see a green light, they should wait for the aircraft to clear the glare and then fire a red pyrotechnic; after a short interval fire a second one. If the search aircraft sees the reds he will turn towards the first one and check his course on the second one, at the same time firing a succession of green lights until he is overhead. The survivors should conserve their pyrotechnics, and only fire a third red signal when the aircraft is almost overhead or is going off course.

SHELTER

35. In the winter you cannot stay in the open and expect to live, unless you are on the move. You must have shelter even if it is only a hole in the snow. Shelter is less important in summer, but it will provide comfort and relaxation under the most ideal conditions. The type of shelter you elect to build will depend on:—

    (a) What tools are available.

    (b) What materials are available.

    (c) What you need shelter from—wind, snow, cold, rain, or insects.

    (d) How long you expect to remain in that location.

Regardless of the type, the shelter must provide adequate ventilation to prevent carbon monoxide poisoning and to allow moisture to escape.

Selection of Site

36. A summer camp site should not be on low-lying ground, which is likely to be damp, or on areas that might be flooded. Select a spot in a cool breeze to keep the insects away, either on top of a ridge, or the shores of a cold lake, or a place that gets an onshore breeze. The lee of boulders and shelving rocks should provide dry camp sites.

37. During winter, protection from the wind is a prime consideration. Avoid the lee of slopes and cliffs where snow may drift heavily and bury your shelter.

38. In mountain camp sites avoid areas which you suspect are subject to avalanches, floods, and rockfalls. Temperature inversions are common in the Arctic so do not camp on a valley floor; it may be several degrees warmer on the slopes.

39. If on sea ice, the site must be on the thickest ice, the biggest floe, and away from thin ice joining two floes where pressure ridges may form.

40. With all sites the nearness to fuel and water must be considered. An ideal camp site is seldom found, and a compromise may be necessary. A site which does not give protection from the wind can be protected by a windbreak. Other deficiencies of a camp site may be similarly overcome.

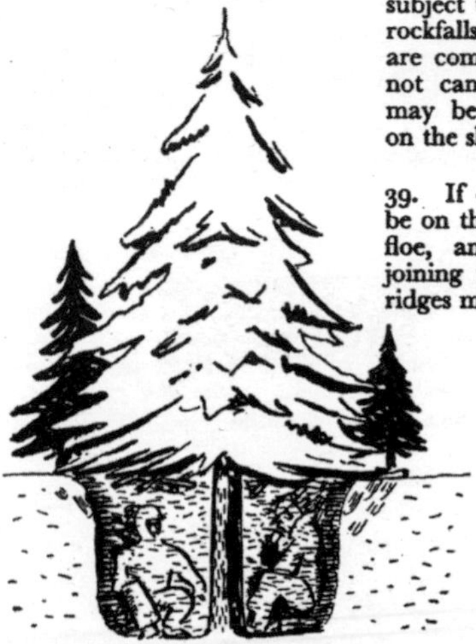

Fig. 4.   Natural Hole under a Tree converted into a Shelter

Natural Shelters

41. Caves and overhanging rockshelves will often provide dry shelters. They should be used in the winter only if well insulated, and in summer only if they can be made insect-proof. In timbered country where the snow is deep, spruce trees often provide ready-made shelters. The natural hole under the lower branches will provide a quickly available shelter. The lower branches at snow level will form the roof. (Fig. 4.)

Aeroplane Shelters

42. In the summer the fuselage will make an adequate shelter if it is on safe ground; it is waterproof and can be made insect-proof with parachutes. It SHOULD NOT be used as a shelter in winter unless it is well insulated. The metal is a good conductor of heat and will quickly dissipate any available heat. In winter you can make two types of shelters using a wing or tailplane as a roof or support. The first, a snow block shelter, is made by piling up snow blocks to form a windbreak, walled shelter, or snow-house. The second is made by hanging engine covers or a parachute over the wing. The loose ends can be anchored by rocks or piles of snow.

Fig. 5. Wing-Snowblock Shelter

19

Parachute Shelters

43. **Paratepee.** An excellent shelter for protection against drizzly weather and insects is made from a parachute canopy. In it you can build a fire, cook, eat, sleep, dress, and make signals—all without going out of doors. You will need ten good poles about 12 to 14 feet long, and half a parachute canopy. The method of construction is shown in the illustrations. The other half of the canopy can be used as additional tenting to provide insulation, should the weather demand it.

Fig. 6. Construction of Paratepee

44. **Pup Tent.** A simple pup tent can be made by placing a rope or pole between two trees or stakes and draping a parachute over it. Stretch the corners down and secure them with stones or pegs.

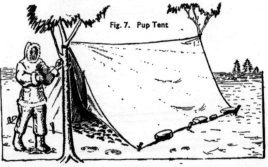

Fig. 7. Pup Tent

45. Simple Bell Tents. A variety of bell tents can be constructed. Always use the double layer principle to provide adequate insulation.

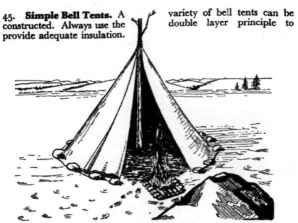

Fig. 8. Simple Parachute Shelter

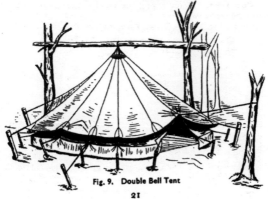

Fig. 9. Double Bell Tent

46. Willow Shelter. Where willows are plentiful this shelter can be made very quickly. The floor area should just accommodate the sleeping bags and the maximum height should just allow the occupants to sit up without their heads touching the roof. The tunnel-like construction is shown in Fig. 10. The framework can be covered with several layers of parachute canopy, which may be anchored with snow.

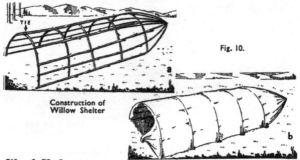

Fig. 10.

Construction of Willow Shelter

Wood Shelters

47. Lean-to and Bough Shelters. If you are in timbered country and have plenty of wood, the best shelter is a lean-to.

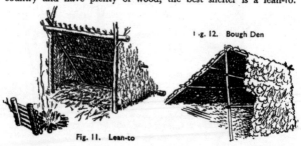

Fig. 12. Bough Den

Fig. 11. Lean-to

22

A good three-man lean-to is shown in Fig. 11. The roof can be covered by sod blocks, spruce boughs, or any suitable material salvaged from the aircraft. Spruce tips and similar materials should be woven in from the top like a tiled roof to prevent rain from entering the shelter. A quickly improvized temporary shelter is a two-sided bough den (Fig. 12); it requires fewer poles and less time to build than a lean-to, but it cannot be water-proofed as efficiently.

Snow Shelters

48. The type of snow shelter you can construct will depend on the quality of the snow. You will have to decide whether or not the snow is suitable for cutting up into snow blocks. The ideal snow for snow block shelters is that upon which a man can walk without breaking through or leaving deeply embedded footprints. The snow must also be tested by pressing a probe into it slowly; if it goes in evenly the snow is ideal for cutting snow blocks. Snow blocks should measure about 18 inches wide by 30 inches long and four to eight inches thick. Blocks of this size should be easy to cut and handle. They will be thick enough to provide good insulation and strength, yet thin enough to allow maximum penetration of the sun's rays. The lighter the interior the warmer it will be and fuel will not have to be used for light. In addition, a light inside a snow block shelter makes a good beacon at night.

49. **Snow Trench.** The ideal snow block shelter is the snow trench, which is designed for one man. Start the construction by marking out a rectangular floor area; big enough to accommodate only one sleeping bag. Remove the snow from this area, by cutting out snow blocks, to the full width of the trench and to a depth of four feet. Along the top edges of the sides of the trench, cut an L-shaped step six inches deep and six inches wide; these steps serve as a base for the snow blocks when the trench is roofed. At the end away from the entrance, place two blocks on the steps on each side of the trench and lean them together to start forming an inverted V roof. The two blocks should be offset, so that after the first pair of blocks are joined, it will be necessary to handle only one block at a time. Each end of the roof should be covered

with blocks and an entrance dug through the snow at the downwind end. If the snow is not four feet deep, the walls can be constructed of snow blocks to the required height.

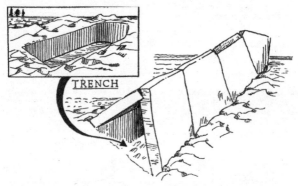

Fig. 13. Construction of Snow Trench

50. **Snow Caves and Snow Holes.**

(*a*) A snow cave can be dug wherever snowdrifts of sufficient depth can be found. Caves are difficult to dig without getting wet and are therefore less desirable than a trench-type shelter. The roof of the cave should be arched to allow moisture to run down the walls without dripping. Also, an arched ceiling will not sag readily from the weight of the snow above.

(*b*) An excellent temporary shelter can be constructed by simply digging a hole in the snow and using your parachute canopy as a roof.

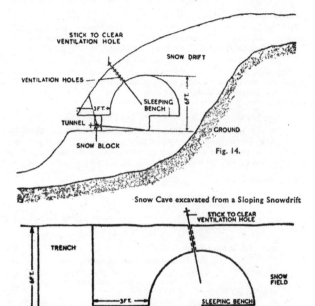

Snow Cave excavated from a Sloping Snowdrift

Snow Cave dug from the Side of a Trench in a Flat Snowfield

51. Big crews should build individual or two-man snow shelters radiating from a central or communal entrance. The entrance can be protected by a circular snow wall and tented with a parachute canopy.

25

Beds and Bedding

52. In snow shelters beds should be made on a sleeping bench which will raise you into the warmer air of the shelter. In all types of shelters beds should be well insulated from the actual floor of the shelter. Depending on your resources the following make good insulating material:—

(a) Parachute canopy, backpad, or seat cushion.

(b) Inverted dinghy.

(c) Lifejacket.

(d) Seat cushions, asbestos, etc., from the aircraft.

(e) Ferns, shrubs, lichens, moss, evergreen boughs (particularly spruce tips).

Your insulating can be as thick as time permits; six inches at least is desirable. Rearrange it regularly to prevent it packing down.

Practical Hints

53. The following points should not be neglected:—

(a) The smaller the shelter the warmer it will be.

(b) Adequate ventilation to prevent asphyxiation and carbon monoxide poisoning is of vital importance.

(c) Two ventilation holes, one near the top of the shelter and the other at the entrance, must be kept clear. One ventilation hole is not sufficient, as the air cannot then circulate

(d) Shovels and tools must be taken into snow shelters, as it may often be necessary to dig a way out if snowfalls or drifting occur.

(e) The entrance of each shelter must be clearly marked so that it can easily be found.

(f) A mark should be made on the snow above each shelter to show its position and to prevent men from walking over the roof.

(g) Drips in snow shelters can be stopped by putting a piece of snow on the source of the drip.

(h) The roof should be at least twelve inches thick unless the snow is very hard, when six inches may be sufficient.

(j) Snow floors should be well tramped down before starting to build the shelter.

FIRES AND EMERGENCY STOVES

54. During survival you are kept warm by a combination of body heat, insulative clothing, and shelter. However, you will need a fire to prepare hot food and drinks in order to maintain and replenish your body heat. A fire is also necessary for drying clothes, for signalling, and to provide external heat. In extreme cold, however, very little heat can be obtained from a fire unless you get so close that you are liable to scorch your clothing. A fire will increase your morale, particularly during the long dark winter days.

55. Your immediate source of heat for cooking is supplied by the emergency stove in the aircraft survival pack; however, this will not be available should you bale out. Your personal survival pack contains candles, which are most suitable for heating snow shelters, fire-making tablets, and matches. These immediate sources of heat may be supplemented, according to your natural fuel supply, by open fires and improvized stoves.

Fires

56. The main ingredients for a good open fire are a good fireplace, kindling, fuel, and a means of lighting the kindling. To these can be added a little knowledge and a lot of patience.

Fig. 16. Log Platform for Fire

Fig. 17. Log Reflector for Fire

57. Fireplaces. Prepare the location of your fires carefully. Don't build a fire under a snow-covered tree—snow may fall and put out the fire. Protect domestic

fires from the wind, and so save fuel. Build the fires on a firm platform; use green logs, stones, cowlings, or dig down to firm soil. Cooking fires should be walled in by green logs or stones, not only to concentrate the heat but to provide a platform for your cooking pot. Fires for warming shelters should be built against a reflector of rocks or green logs to direct the heat into the shelter.

Fig. 18. Cooking Platform

58. Kindling. You will need some easily inflammable kindling to get a fire going. Pick up kindling whenever you can find it, even if you do not expect to make camp for some hours. Gather birch bark, dry lichens, twigs, resinous shrubs, bits of fat (if not required for food), feathers, tufts of dry grass and sedges, against the possibility of a shortage of good kindling at the camp site. Larger twigs can be cut in "feather fashion" if kindling is scarce.

Fig. 19. Birch Bark Under-layers   Fig. 20. Feathering Wood for Tinder

28

Paper or rags and twigs soaked in fuel or oil are good artificial kindling.

59. **Natural Fuel.**

(a) *Wood.* Even in polar regions there are clumps of dwarf willow and birch. Birch is oily and if split fine will burn even if wet. Standing deadwood and dead branches provide your best fuel; the dead trees can be easily pushed over and chopped up. Lying deadwood and driftwood is likely to be frozen or waterlogged and is useless unless dried out. Green timber can be burned on a hot fire.

(b) *Coal.* Outcrops may be found occasionally on the surface and coal may be found washed up on beaches.

(c) *Animal Fats.* Use animal fats for food rather than fuel. You will derive more heat from fat you eat than from fat you burn.

(d) *Gassiope.* In some barren grounds, where there is no driftwood and little willow or birch, the Eskimos depend almost entirely on this plant for fuel. It is a low, spreading, evergreen plant, with tiny leaves and white bell-shaped flowers. It grows from four to twelve inches high and contains so much resin that it will burn even when green or wet.

(e) In treeless areas you can find other natural fuels such as dry grass which can be twisted into bunches, peat dry enough to burn (found at the top of undercut river banks), and dried animal dung. Try anything for fuel, but in small quantities until you are certain of its qualities.

Firelighting

60. Get all your materials together before you try to start the fire. Make sure your kindling and fuel are dry, and have enough fuel on hand to keep the fire going. Arrange a small amount of kindling in a low pyramid, close enough together to allow the flames to lick from one piece to another. Leave a small opening for lighting. Save matches by using a candle to light the fire, or make a faggot of thin dry twigs tied loosely. Apply the lighted candle or faggot to the lower windward side of the kindling, shielding it from the wind as you do so. Use the firemaking tablets only

Light your fire with a candle —

note correct way to lay fire.

Fig. 21.   Laying a Fire

if the tinder is damp. Small pieces of wood or other fuel can be laid gently on the kindling before lighting, or can be added as the kindling begins to burn. Add larger pieces of fuel when the kindling pile is considered large enough to support and ignite them. Don't pack the wood so tight that the draught is shut off. Encourage the fire by blowing gently on it.

61.   For a large fire, the sticks in each layer should be parallel to each other and at right angles to the layer below. Space the sticks so that the air can get between them and create a good draught. For a small fire lay the sticks in radial fashion, and as they burn push them into the fire. With this method longer sticks need not be chopped up.

Emergency Fire Lighting

62.   The availability of fire-lighting equipment may mean success or failure in a fight for survival. Many people have lost their lives because they have been unable to light a fire to provide warmth or attract attention. Your personal survival kit provides matches, candles, firemaking tablets, and a magnifying glass for this purpose.

63.   Firemaking without matches requires bone-dry tinder which will burn very easily. Very dry powdered wood, finely shredded dry bark, cotton, twine, first-aid gauze bandage, fuzzy or woolly material scraped from plants, fine bird's feathers, or bird's nests are most suitable. You can make it burn more easily by adding a few drops of fuel.

64.   **Burning Lens.** An emergency burning lens may be obtained from binoculars, gunsights, bombsights, or cameras. The lens should be used to focus the sun's rays on the timber.

65. Flint and Steel. A flint and steel is the easiest and most reliable way of making fire without matches. Your knife and sharpening stone or a piece of hard rock should produce a good spark. Hold the flint as near to the tinder as possible; strike it with a sharp scraping downward motion so that the sparks fall into the centre of the tinder.

Fig. 22. Lighting a Fire with Flint and Steel

66. Bow Drill. Another standby is the bow drill. This consists of a bow made from a willow strung with some cord made from your parachute shroud lines. The drill is a circular shaft of dry wood around which the bow string is wound once. The drill shaft is pointed at one end and round at the other. The round end revolves in a depression made in a piece of wood which is held in one hand. Lubricate this depression. The point of the drill is placed in a notch in another piece of wood, which is filled with tinder. By holding the drill shaft in position and moving the bow

Note notch.

Fig. 23. Bow and Drill Method of Firemaking

back and forth in a sawing motion in a horizontal plane, friction is set up and the tinder ignited.

57. **Pyrotechnic.** A pyrotechnic may have to be used to light a fire if all other means have failed. Weigh the use of the pyrotechnic as an emergency signal against the need of a fire. The powder extracted from a pyrotechnic will burn so quickly that it will be necessary to mix a slower burning material with it; powdered wood or shredded fabrics are the best mixing materials. The powder from one pyrotechnic will provide sufficient tinder for a number of fires. The unused powder should be kept dry. Above all, **be extremely careful when you are extracting the powder from the pyrotechnic.**

Stockpile

68. Make all your preparations as far ahead as possible, regardless of whether or not you have been located. Stockpile fuel against bad weather or shortages. Stack it where it cannot be lost by drifting snow and protect it from rain. Prepare your kindling at least three fires ahead and store it inside your shelter.

Improvised Stoves

69. Aircraft fuels such as rubber, wax insulation, fuel and oil are more economically burned in improvised stoves. These stoves can be used inside or outside the shelter as required. To burn petrol, place one or two inches of sand or fine gravel in a tin or similar container and saturate it with petrol. Make slots at the top of the can to let the flames and smoke out and punch holes just above the level of the sand to provide a draught. To make the fire burn longer mix some oil with the petrol. If you have no container dig a hole in the ground, fill it with sand or gravel and pour on the fuel. Be careful when lighting; the petrol may explode; protect your face and hands. Lubricating oil, kerosene, or animal fats will not burn directly, but you can use them with a wick arrangement. Make a wick of kapok, asbestos, rope, rag, etc., and support it in the oil with a wire frame. A very simple stove can be made by putting a candle in a ventilated tin can. This will provide all the heat required for a snow shelter. (Figs. 24 and 25.)

Fig. 24.
Improvised Petrol Stove

Fig. 25.
Improvised Stove using Wick
to burn Oil or Animal Fat

Ventilation

70. The need for proper ventilation cannot be over-emphasized. When open fires or stoves are burned inside shelters, carbon monoxide and other gases will accumulate unless the shelter is ventilated. Also if animal fats or oil are burned, good ventilation will carry away the heavy black smoke. If a vent is made in the lower portion of the shelter—the entrance should be sufficient—and another at the top, cold air will move in through the lower opening, be warmed, and pass out through the top vent. The current of air will carry away the carbon monoxide and soot. Remember that carbon monoxide is heavier than air and a man lying down will be first affected. To retain the maximum amount of heat in a shelter restrict the vent holes when fires are out. *Restrict the temptation to "get up a good fug".*

FOOD

71. Take stock of all your available food. Your emergency food packs and uneaten flying rations are your immediate, and in the barren lands probably your only, sources of food. Your

food pack has been designed to provide sustenance for three days' very hard work, five days' active work, or seven days' normal work. The food packs contain their own directions of how they should be used. In extreme cold, two hot meals a day are necessary; one for breakfast and the other in the evening. Also, if you have enough, a hot drink at midday is desirable. Avoid drinking two hours before bedding down and remember to urinate immediately before getting into your sleeping bag.

Living Off the Land

72. Contrary to general belief, food is not abundant in the Arctic. All wild life is migratory and, since neither the time nor the position of the crash can be predetermined, there is no point in attempting to take up the involved subject of seasonal game distribution. The game you get in survival will either be there or come there. It means that you should survey the locality, set suitable traps, and wait for the game to come. To get food from the land you will have to do some very determined foraging. Leave a man in the camp at all times as look-out, while the rest of the party searches for food; detail men for fishing or hunting according to their talents. Care should be taken to blaze a trail back to camp. In large aircraft you might be carrying some sort of firearm, but you will normally have to rely on the snares and fishing kits in your survival packs. Additional snares may be made from wire and parachute elastics salvaged from the crash. You will have to learn where to look, what to look for, and, in all except plant food, how to catch it. When you find local animal or plant food, eat as much as you want and save your emergency rations. Fat is heat-producing food and very important to your health in the Arctic. Eat a lot of fat only when you can drink at least two pints of water daily. If you have any doubt about the safety of any wild food use the following rule: eat a spoonful and wait eight hours; if there are no ill effects, such as vomiting or diarrhoea, eat a handful and wait another eight hours. If there are still no ill effects, you can eat reasonable quantities safely.

Animal Food

73. Finding animals on the open tundra is not easy, but don't be too quick in deciding that the area is lifeless. Keep on the lookout for any signs of animal life—such as excrement, tracks,

hair, and, in extremely cold weather, "animal smoke" steaming from their bodies. These may put you on the trail of food. Wherever there is one kind of animal there are almost sure to be other forms of life. The animals you may find range from lemmings, which are stub-tailed mice, to polar bears. What you catch will depend on your facilities and skill. Small animals such as lemmings, muskrats, hares, woodchucks, squirrels, and snowshoe rabbits, can be caught with sling shots, snares, deadfalls, and other simple traps. The larger animals such as polar and brown bears, caribou, moose, seals, mountain sheep, and wolverine, are difficult to kill. They may be snared or captured by deadfalls and pit traps, but unless they are strangled or stunned they are hard to kill without a gun. Learn to attract animals by kissing the back of your hand vigorously and making a squeaking noise which indicates the presence of a wounded mouse or bird; that should definitely attract some hungry animal. But learn to conceal yourself.

Fig. 26. Simple Deadfall

Fig. 27. Tripwire Deadfall

Fig. 28. Simple Snare

Fig. 29. Trigger Snare

35

74. **Hunting Hints.**

(*a*) Keep the wind in your face. A calm day is not generally windless; make sure of the wind direction.

(*b*) Try to have the sun in your back, especially a rising or setting sun.

(*c*) In timber country move slowly and carefully; don't break any twigs under foot or allow swinging branches to hit your clothing.

(*d*) In hilly and mountainous country big game animals generally watch them below them more than above. Keep slightly above the level where the game is most likely to be seen.

(*e*) In mountainous country, cross currents make it less important to keep the wind in your face.

(*f*) Animals are used to rolling stones in the mountains, therefore it is not quite so important to avoid noise.

(*g*) Avoid crispy snow; try to hunt where snow is soft.

(*h*) Don't expose yourself against a skyline.

(*j*) Never stay on the game trail; all wild game watch their back trails.

(*k*) If game is feeding, you can attempt to approach it by stalking in the open. Crawl slowly when all heads are down. Freeze motionless—whatever your position—the instant an animal starts to raise its head.

(*l*) When shooting game aim for the vital areas: behind the ears, in the throat, or behind the foreshoulders. Much game is lost because it is out of range.

75. **Poisonous Animals.** The liver of polar bears and bearded seals is poisonous at certain times of the year and should not be eaten. Rabbits are generally so lean and have so little food value that to get enough energy out of them you have to eat a little too much for comfort. Try to supplement your diet with other things.

Bird Food

76. Many northern birds nest in colonies which may run to hundreds of thousands of pairs. Near such a colony a man can keep alive—even without a gun. Some Arctic birds are well

supplied with fats—notably ducks, geese, and swans. These water birds all go through a two- or three-week flightless period while they are moulting in midsummer. The best known winter birds are the ptarmigan or snow partridge, which is rarely fat; the white owl, which is usually fat and tasty; and the raven, which is tough. All birds are good to eat cooked or raw. Their blood and livers are edible. The feathers can be used for insulation. The entrails and toes make good bait.

77. **Bird Catching.** Study bird habits closely. Hunt for birds on their meeting grounds on islands, cliffs, marshes and lakes, on coastal plains, and on flats in interior areas. An improvized slingshot is a good bird catcher. Ptarmigan are very tame and can be killed with a stick or stone. Gulls can be caught with a gorge hook and line; bait the hook and let it float on a piece of wood or stake it out on a beach. Eskimos set a simple noose snare in the nest itself to catch the bird's feet.

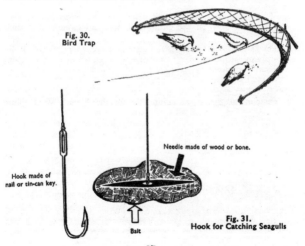

Fig. 30.
Bird Trap

Needle made of wood or bone.

Hook made of
nail or tin-can key.

Bait

Fig. 31.
Hook for Catching Seagulls

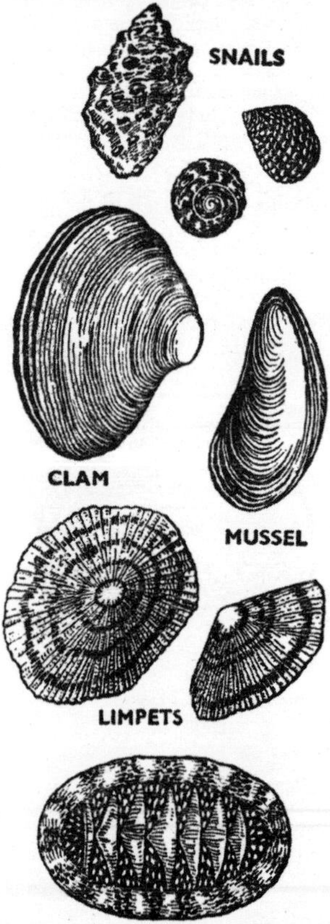

Fish Food

78. The deeper streams, rivers, lakes, and tidal pools are all worth fishing. Along most Arctic shores clams, mussels, snails, limpets, chitons, sea urchins, and sea cucumbers, are plentiful. Don't eat shellfish that you find dead. Live shellfish move when touched or cling tightly to the rocks. The small blackish-purple mussel in Northern Pacific waters is poisonous at certain times of the year and should not be eaten. The chief characteristics of poisonous fish is that they lack ordinary scales, and instead have either a naked skin or are encased in a bony box-like covering or are covered with bristles, spiney scales, strong sharp thorns, or spines. Others puff up like a balloon on being taken out of the water. Cooking does not destroy the poisonous alkaloids in these fish. Never eat a fish that has slimy gills, sunken eyes, flabby flesh or skin, or an unpleasant odour. If on pressing the thumb against the fish it remains deeply dented, the fish is probably stale and should not be eaten. Avoid all types of jelly fish.

SNAILS

CLAM

MUSSEL

LIMPETS

CHITON

Fig. 32.   Edible Seafood   38

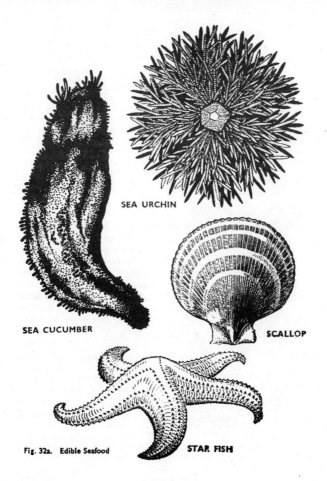

SEA URCHIN

SEA CUCUMBER

SCALLOP

Fig. 32a. Edible Seafood

STAR FISH

79. Fishing Equipment. The fishing gear in your survival kit is not your only means of catching fish. They can be speared, caught in improvised nets, or stunned with sticks and stones. In shallow water you can even catch them with your hands. Those who have a fish net, or know how to make one and use it properly, will catch the most fish. Remember that a net works twenty-four hours a day.

80. Line Fishing. In addition to your fishing kit, hooks can be made from stiff wire or tin openers, and lines from the inner cords of your parachute shroud lines. Another effective device is a fishing needle of wood or bone sunk in bait (see Fig. 31). The needle is swallowed whole and a pull on the line swings it crosswise, causing it to catch in the fish's stomach or gullet. Use the least appetising parts of animals and birds for bait. A white stone used for a sinker, or a bit of shiny metal or brightly coloured piece of material tied just above the hook will also attract fish.

(a) **Jigging.** Fish may be caught by jigging for them. Let the hook, or a cluster of hooks attached below a "spoon" or shiny metal, down into deep water. Jerk it upwards at arm's length, and let it sink back. If you are fishing in deep water, be sure the hooks are weighted enough to

Fig. 33. Improvised Fish-hooks 40

carry the lure downwards quickly so that it suggests something alive.

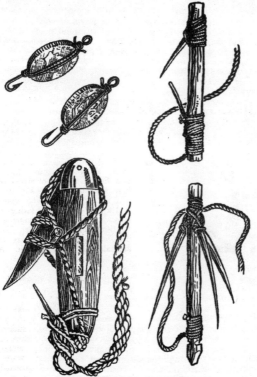

Fig. 33a. Improvised Fish-hooks

81. Narrowing a Stream. To catch fish, a shallow stream may be narrowed by building an obstruction of stones or stakes out from both banks, leaving only a narrow channel through which the fish can swim. An improvised net is stretched across this channel; be sure to secure it firmly with stakes or boulders or you will lose both net and fish. If you have no net, you can stand ready to hit, spear, or trap, the fish as they swim past. Keep very still while you wait—fish dart away at the first sign of danger.

82. Diverting a Stream. If you are certain that a small stream has fish in it, divert it and so strand fish in the pools in the stream below the diversion.

83. Tidal Fish Trap. To strand fish when the tide goes out, pile up a crescent of boulders on the tidal flat. Scooping out the area inside the crescent is not essential, but increases the effectiveness of the trap.

 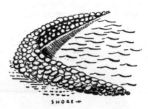

MAZE TYPE FISH TRAP   **TIDAL FLAT FISH TRAP**

Fig. 34. Tidal Fish Traps

84. White Fish Traps. If you come across a lagoon, select a spot about eight feet from it and two feet below water level. Dig a hole four feet in diameter, and join the hole to the lagoon with a trench about two feet wide, and deep enough to allow four inches of water to flow easily through the channel from the lagoon. Place a small log about three inches in diameter where the channel drops into the hole and fill the trench in behind it to smooth the

42

channel bed. Sit where the fish cannot see you and wait. Soon the fish will feel the current and, thinking that it will be taking them out to sea, allow it to carry them over the artificial falls into your pools.

85. **Fish in Tidal Pools.** Tidal pools with masses of seaweed in them may seem to contain no fish, but you may find small fish among the seaweed near the surface and a few big ones deeper down. For the small fish you will need a scoop or net. For the big ones use a spear or fish catcher.

86. **Fishing through Ice.** The main deterrent when attempting to fish through ice is thickness of the ice; it may be as much as 12 feet thick. Fishing with a hook and line through a hole in the ice requires no special technique, but setting a net beneath ice requires skill and patience. To set a net under ice, the float line may be fed under the ice by using a series of holes in the ice, one or two long poles, and a leader line tied to the float line. Fish get caught by entangling themselves in the mesh, therefore the net should be fairly loosely tied to the float line to allow some flexibility

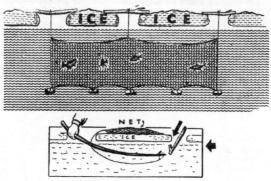

Method of placing net under ice.

Fig. 35. Setting Net under Ice

43

in the meshes. The net may be supported in the water by a combination of poles, floats, and ropes. Weights, made of almost anything, should be tied on to the bottom line.

Plant Food

87. Though plant food is not abundant in the Arctic, it is by no means absent. There are many varieties of berries, greens, roots, fungi, lichens, and seaweeds, which can be used as emergency food. In forested areas, food plants are most abundant in clearings, and along streams and seashores. On the tundra they are largest and most plentiful in wet places. Don't be discouraged by the bare appearance of northern vegetation; food is often hidden. Watch the feeding habits of animals, particularly birds; they will lead you to plants you might otherwise overlook. If you are on the march, gather food plants as you go along so that you will have enough for a meal by the time you make camp.

88. **Poisonous Plants.** Generally speaking, do not eat plants which taste bitter or have a milky sap. The following poisonous plants grow in the sub-Arctic forests; they do not normally grow north of the tree line:—

Fig. 36. Deathcup Amanita
—Poisonous

(a) **Mushrooms.** The common characteristics of the two species of poisonous mushrooms are that they have white gills and swollen or bulbous bases. The nutritive value of mushrooms is very small, and unless you are an expert they are best left well alone. There is a possibility that the very young of the deadly amanita mushroom family may be mistaken for a puff ball. By cutting the ball in half you can make certain. If gills are found inside throw it away: no true puff balls have gills.

44

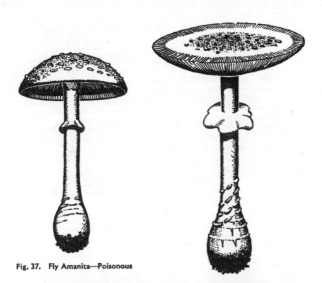

Fig. 37. Fly Amanita—Poisonous

(b) *Water Hemlock.* The water hemlock grows in the wet soil of river valleys in forested areas. On an average the plant is four feet tall, but in favourable locations it grows to six to eight feet tall. The arrangement of the flowers is a conspicuous characteristic which enables you to recognize immediately the members of this family (the parsley or carrot family). The root is hollow and has cross partitions. The leaves are streaked with purple and when crushed emit a disagreeable odour. (Fig. 38.)

(c) *Baneberry.* The berries are usually red or white but may turn blue as they get older. It can be distinguished from the edible blueberry by the fact that baneberry bushes carry their fruits in clusters and have big leaves made up of several parts; edible blueberries grow singly. (Fig. 39.)

45

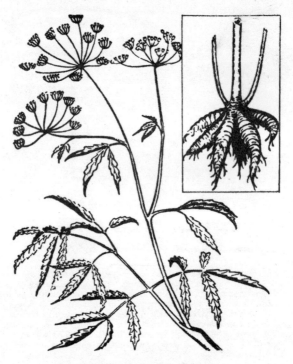

Fig. 38. Water Hemlock—Poisonous

Fig. 39. Baneberry—Poisonous

47

Cooking

89. Whenever possible, cook your food before eating it. Meals should be prepared in sheltered places. Windbreaks and large stones should be used to protect the flame and reflect the heat. Hot embers provide the most heat.

90. Since fuel is usually scarce, it is advisable to cook by means of boiling, and if possible drink the cooking water. Boiling in water is the easiest and most satisfactory method of preparing fish and game under survival conditions. Boiling preserves the essential elements of the food. It is best to boil sea food in sea water; no additional salting is then required. Undercook rather than overcook; it saves vitamins and heat. Boil for two or three minutes only. Plant foods should be mixed with other foods in stews and soups. Lichens are most edible when soaked overnight, dried until brittle, crushed into a powder, and then boiled until they form a jelly. The jelly will make an excellent base for any soup or stew.

91. When a cooking pot is not available, in winter the food may be roasted or fried over a slow, non-smoking fire; in summer the food is best cooked by wrapping it in clay or mud and wet leaves, and baked in hot embers. When food is baked it should not be skinned or cleaned until it is cooked.

92. If no fire is available food becomes more palatable if dried or frozen. Before eating frozen food it should be brought to a temperature a few degrees below freezing since, when very cold, the frozen food sticks to the lips and tongue. When carved or sliced into thin shavings, it is really palatable and does not appear raw.

Food Storage

93. Your food supply—especially fresh meat—will attract thieving animals. Another problem is the alternate freezing and thawing which is bad for any food. In winter let your food freeze and stay frozen until you need it. It is not necessary to thaw before cooking. Frozen food may take a little longer to cook, but otherwise it is unaffected. In summer, your fish can be cut into strips and dried in the sun; meat and game should be kept in a cool

place in the shade. Newly-killed meat or game should be tied in a parachute cloth to keep out flies which otherwise will lay eggs on the meat. A hole dug in the shady side of an embankment, with a wet piece of heavy material hung over the entrance, will give a small degree of refrigeration. A hole dug in the ground similarly covered will also make a good refrigerator. On the tundra a common method of storing food is to place it beneath a pile of boulders. If boulders are not available bury your food in the snow, and mark the spot. In timbered country, if it becomes necessary for every one to be away from the camp (one man should be left to operate the emergency signals) don't leave the food where animals can reach it. Tie it in a bundle and hang it from a tree at least six feet from the ground and a foot or two from the branches.

WATER

94. Your water supply will be limited only by the amount of heat available for melting snow and ice. In an effort to save fuel men deprive themselves of drinking water. Inefficiency, exhaustion and dehydration may occur through lack of water, even in the Arctic. Drink if possible two pints of water daily. The water lost through the sweat glands, and in the form of urine, must be replaced. The amount of water lost in the form of sweat, and therefore your requirements, can be limited by regulating your rate of work and removing some of your clothing whenever you begin to feel warm.

95. In summer, water can be obtained from streams, lakes, or ponds. On the tundra, pond water may be brown because of stain from grass roots and other plants, but it is fit to drink.

96. In winter, your water supply is most easily obtained from lakes under the ice and snow. The lower surface of the ice follows the contours of the top surface of the snow; dig where the snow is deepest and then chip through the ice under this to find the least cold water. Melt ice rather than snow for water; you will get more water for volume and it takes less time and heat. The deeper layers of snow are more granular and give a better yield of water then the soft upper snow. When melting snow, place

a small amount in the pot at first, adding more as it melts. If you fill the pot with snow, the first water will be soaked up by the absorbent snow above it, leaving a cavity directly over the heated bottom of the pot and the pot will burn.

97. At sea you can obtain good drinking water from old sea ice. Ice a year old rarely has any noticeable saltiness, while ice two or three years' old is generally fresher than the average river or spring water. Old sea ice can be distinguished from the current year's ice by its rounded corners and bluish colour, in contrast to the rougher sea ice which has a milky grey colour. In summer, drinking water can be obtained from pools in the old sea ice. Avoid pools near the edge of the floe where salt water may have blown in.

98. **Purification of Water.** If there is any doubt as to the quality of the water you intend to drink or cook with, it should be purified by one of the following methods:—

(a) *Halazone Tablets.* Crunch and dissolve one halazone tablet in each pint of water. Shake well and allow to stand for half-an-hour. If this is insufficient to produce a distinct smell of chlorine, add more halazone until the odour is present.

(b) *Boiling.* Boil the water for at least three minutes and allow any sediment to settle before using.

HEALTH HAZARDS

Hypothermia

99. Hypothermia is the condition existing when the body temperature is below normal. Low temperature, winds, and dampness, supplement each other in depleting the body's heat resources to produce a sub-normal temperature. Hypothermia may be recognized by decreasing resistance to cold, excessive shivering, and low vitality.

100. The treatment consists of returning the body temperature to normal. The patient should be put in his sleeping bag, or a bed improvized from a parachute canopy, the buttocks, shoulders, and feet, being well insulated. The patient should be warmed by

placing heated rocks, wrapped in some material, near the various parts of the body. If the number of heating units is limited place them as far as they will go in this order: pit of the stomach, small of the back, armpits, back of the neck, wrists, and between the thighs. Stimulation with hot drinks will also help if the patient is conscious. Avoid the use of alcohol; it opens the blood vessels at the surface of the skin allowing heat to be lost more rapidly. A victim of hypothermia is not cured when his body temperature returns to normal. Build up his reserve of body heat. To prevent hypothermia take all possible measures to conserve body heat.

Frostbite

101. **Areas Most Affected.** Frostbite affects particularly the exposed parts of the body and regions which are farthest from the heart and have the least blood circulation, *i.e.* the face, nose, ears, hands, and feet.

102. **Prevention.** To avoid frostbite remember these precautions:—

(*a*) Keep wrinkling your face to make sure that stiff patches have not formed. Watch your hands.

(*b*) Watch each others' faces and ears for signs of frostbite.

(*c*) Don't handle cold metal with bare hands.

(*d*) Avoid tight clothing which will reduce circulation and increase the risk of frostbite.

(*e*) Avoid exposure in high winds.

(*f*) Avoid spilling petrol on bare flesh. Petrol-splashed flesh in sub-zero temperatures will freeze almost at once.

(*g*) Do not go out of your shelter, even for short periods, without adequate clothing.

(*h*) Take special care if you are unfit or fatigued; the risk then increases.

(*j*) Don't let your clothing become wet from sweat or water. If it does, dry it promptly.

103. **Symptoms.**

(*a*) Frostbite first appears as a small patch of white or cream-coloured frozen skin, which is firm to the touch and feels stiff. Frostbite can be felt by making faces and moving all the skin on the face and forehead. The subject may feel a slight

Fig. 40. Making Faces to Prevent Frostbite

pricking sensation as the skin freezes, or may not notice it at all. If treatment is given at this stage the consequences will not be serious; but if the process goes further, the deeper tissues of muscle and bone are frozen, the blood vessels become clotted, and so much tissue may be destroyed that part of a limb, an ear, or a nose, may be lost.

(*b*) If the frostbite is quite mild, when the area is warmed up, there will be some swelling and redness of the skin with a little pain and, as the condition heals, the skin may scale off.

(*c*) If the bite is deeper and more serious, swelling and pain are marked and blisters form. These may become infected, forming ulcers, and in the worst case the tissues become grey, then black and dead. Such tissues will fall off eventually.

52

104. **Treatment.** Careful and immediate attention must be given.

(a) Very slight cases may be treated by simply getting out of the wind. A small area may be warmed by placing a bare hand over it, covering the outside of the hand with its mitt. The woollen pads on the backs of the mitts may provide enough warmth in some cases.

(b) Frostbitten hands should be thrust inside your clothing against your body.

(c) Frostbitten feet should be thrust inside a companion's clothing if you are out in the open.

(d) Keep the part covered with dry clothing until you reach shelter.

(e) Never rub frostbite with snow.

(f) In more serious cases the patient will almost certainly require treatment for exposure. Get him to shelter or build a shelter round him.

(g) If blisters appear, do not burst them. Dust them with an antiseptic powder.

(h) Cover the frostbitten parts lightly with surgical dressings, or clean soft clothes. Wrap up the parts loosely.

(i) Never rub a frostbitten area.

(k) Never warm up frostbite quickly by holding before the fire or dipping into hot water, or by any other means. Use "animal" warmth only.

(l) If there is severe pain give morphia if available. Very severe pain is usually an indication that the frostbitten parts have been made too hot and further damage is occurring.

(m) Keep the damaged areas at rest.

Snow Blindness

105. Snow blindness is a temporary form of blindness caused by the high intensity and concentration of the sun's rays, both direct and reflected, from the snow-covered ground or ice and ice crystals in the clouds. However, snow blindness may occur during a bright overcast when there is no direct light, but a bright general haze from all directions. It occurs most frequently when the sun is high, particularly in areas which do not lose their snow cover.

106. Symptoms. First the eyes become sensitive to the glare, then blinking and squinting occurs. Next the landscape takes on a pinkish tinge and the eyes begin to water. Blinking and watering become more intense and the vision becomes redder, until a sensation similar to that of sand in the eyes is noticed. If the exposure is continued the sensation becomes more violent until the vision is blanked out completely by a flaming red curtain. It is impossible to open the eyes or to black the red vision. There is intense pain which may last three or four days.

107. Treatment. The treatment consists of getting the person into a dark place. If there is no dark place available a blindfold may be used. The pain is aggravated by heat and may be relieved by the application of a cool wet compress. Time is the only cure.

108. Prevention. The wearing of the standard goggles in the personal survival kit is recommended. If for some reason you have no goggles, some kind of goggles can be made from wood, bark, cloth or paper; do not use metal. Blackening the skin round the eyes will cut down the number of rays entering the eyes.

Fig. 41. Protection against Snow blindness

54

Carbon Monoxide Poisoning

109. All forms of fires and stoves are liable to give off carbon monoxide gas, and are therefore a potential danger in shelters unless ventilation is adequate (*see* para. 70). Poisoning by these fumes is common in severe cold conditions because of the very natural tendency to batten down closely. The gas is colourless and odourless.

110. The effects of breathing the gas are insidious. There may be slight headache, dizziness, drowsiness, nausea, and perhaps vomiting, but usually these symptoms are very mild and may pass unnoticed, and the subject becomes unconscious without any warning. Unless discovered promptly the subject will die as the effects of the gas increase.

111. The treatment is simple. Remove the patient to a well-ventilated place and encourage him to breath evenly and regularly. If he is unconscious and breathing shallowly, apply artificial respiration. Administer oxygen if available. When he is conscious keep him warm and at rest and give hot drinks. Do not allow him to exert himself until he is fully recovered.

Personal Hygiene

112. Strict attention must be paid to personal cleanliness to prevent skin and intestinal infections which are associated with neglect of personal hygiene.

(*a*) Hair and beards should be trimmed as short as possible. Frost accumulates readily on beards and can only be removed by thawing.

(*b*) Winter survival is not conducive to bathing; however, it is still necessary to remove accumulated body oils and perspiration from the skin. Under severe conditions a dry rubdown is all that is possible; otherwise wash the body with a damp rag.

(*c*) The teeth and mouth should be cleaned daily. Feathers make a good toothpick and several tied together make a reasonable toothbrush. A piece of cloth can also be used.

(*d*) Attend promptly to any tender skin, particularly on the feet. It may prevent real trouble later on.

Camp Hygiene

113. Use a little commonsense when arranging your camp site. Site your lavatory to the leeward of the camp, well away from your shelter and water supply. Clean the camp site regularly, and above all do not contaminate your water supply.

General Health

114. Conserve your energy. Do not rush around aimlessly. Avoid fatigue. Get plenty of sleep. If you cannot sleep, just lie down and relax your body and mind. You will not freeze to death when you sleep unless you are utterly exhausted. If you are doing hard work remove excess clothing before you get hot, and rest as soon as you begin to feel hot, or at least for five minutes in every thirty.

CLOTHING PRECAUTIONS

115. It has previously been stated that your clothing is your first line of defence in Arctic survival, and it follows that care of the clothing is most important. The following points should be particularly observed.

116. **Regulation and Ventilation.** Strange as it may seem, one of the chief causes of freezing to death arises from having become overheated in the first place. Excess body vapour will condense and in extreme cases will freeze. This has two effects: the moisture will destroy the insulating qualities of the underclothing, and the water vapour, being a good conductor of heat, will draw heat from the body. Constantly regulate your clothing so that you do not become hot enough to sweat. This is a considerable nuisance, but absolutely necessary. Slacken off all draw cords, open up the clothing at the neck, and loosen belts to allow ventilation. When necessary, remove enough layers of clothing to keep cool, whether you are indoors or travelling, or working outdoors. Replace the clothing as soon as you start to cool off.

117. **Repairs.** Immediately mend tears and holes, particularly in outer garments which must be windproof.

118. **Drying Out.** Dry your garments as soon as possible if they have become wet. Clothing should be hung high up in shelters to dry, as the warmest air is high up. In emergency, clothing can be dried by body heat, by putting it under your outer clothing or inside your sleeping bag. Mukluks and boucherons should be dried in the open by sublimation, that is, allowing the perspiration to condense and then freeze. The frozen perspiration can then be brushed out.

119. **Fluffing Out.** Compression reduces the fluffiness of a material and hence the volume of insulating air it can contain. Socks must be turned frequently and fluffed out to prevent matting. Insoles should be changed from foot to foot to prevent them always being compressed in the same spot. All other woollen garments should be fluffed out regularly.

120. **Spares for Changing.** If possible carry extra dry clothing for changing, particularly socks. Several layers of the parachute canopy wrapped round your feet are better than wet socks. Dry grass stuffed between the layers provides useful insulation.

121. **Frost Removal.** Remove snow and hoar frost from clothing by beating, shaking and scraping, before entering a warmer atmosphere. Willow canes or a whisk made of spruce tips can be used for this purpose. Snow or frost does not wet clothing unless it is melted by warmth, so if you cannot remove the snow it is better to leave the outer garments where it is cold, so that the snow will not melt.

122. **Snow Contact.** Don't sit down directly on the snow. Your body heat will melt it and your clothing will become wet. Always sit on surplus clothing, a log, or some piece of equipment. Don't put your hands with snow-covered gloves into your pockets. Shake off the snow first.

123. **Tightness of Clothing.** Avoid tight clothing, particularly tight footgear and handwear. Don't try to cram too many pairs of socks into your footgear, because a tight fit is as bad as, if not worse than, insufficient covering.

124. **Cleanliness.** Keep all your clothing as clean as possible. Dirty, matted clothing is less warm. The dirt will fill the space normally occupied by the insulating air.

125. **Gloves.** Don't lose your gloves or mittens. Secure them, by the loops provided, with a neck string.

126. **Taking Chances.** Don't take chances about clothing. Unprotected fingers and ears can be frostbitten in a few minutes.

127. **Sleeping Bags.** Never get into your sleeping bag wearing wet clothing. Sleep in the minimum clothing required for warmth; naked if possible. Turn the bag inside out in the morning and dry it before a fire or by sublimation. When it is dry, reassemble it and roll it up tightly until it is needed again. Don't sleep with your head in the bag, otherwise moist exhaled air will enter the bag. Sleep with your head in the aperture, and cover your face with your necksquare folded up to at least four thicknesses.

128. **Clothing Hints.**

(a) When walking in deep snow, wear your trousers outside your footwear and secure the bottoms of the legs with the draw cords.

(b) If you are unfortunate enough to fall into water, immediately roll yourself in the snow. The snow will act as a blotter and soak up the water. The violent exercise will generate body heat and will also knock off any saturated snow. If possible wring out underclothing, but let the outer clothing freeze to maintain and protect body heat.

(c) Never take off boots filled with water until you are in some form of shelter. As long as water remains liquid there is no danger of frostbite. Walking generates enough heat to prevent solidification for a considerable time even at very low temperatures.

(d) Footwear can be made temporarily waterproof by dipping them, while on the feet, into water, until a film of ice is formed on the outside. The footwear will not let in water until the ice has melted. Coating with ice is an extreme emergency procedure and should never be used if there are other alternatives.

INSECTS

129. From mid-June to mid-September, when the first heavy frosts come, your worst enemies are the insects. During this period, there are ten times as many mosquitos per square mile over two-thirds of the land north of the tree line than in the tropics. Hence the provision of the head net and insect repellant cream in your personal survival kit.

130. There are four insect families: mosquitos, black flies, deer flies, and midges. They do not resemble each other in general appearance, but they are alike in several significant ways:

(a) They all bite, that is, they do not sting.

(b) They do not generally carry disease.

(c) They are primarily daytime insects.

(d) If it turns cold, they become inactive, even when they are abundant.

(e) Only the females bite.

(f) During their larval stage they live in water.

Types

131. (a) *Mosquitos.* Mosquitos need no description; they are universal pests.

(b) *Black Flies.* Sometimes known as sandflies or buffalo gnats. Their bites stay open and will continue to bleed for some time; the bite causes severe swelling. They attack especially at the collar line, and, if they get inside the clothing, at the waist line.

(c) *Deer Flies.* These large pests are also known as gadflies. Other flies in the same family are mooseflies; these are larger still and are also called horseflies or bulldogs. The last name is particularly apt in view of their tenacity and the size of the hole they drill in the skin. Their bite is like the cut of a scalpel, drawing blood in a trickle.

(d) *Midges.* These are minute flies about one twenty-fifth of an inch long; also known as no-see-ums, pinkies, and gnats. They are persistent blood suckers and cause a sharp, burning pain out of all proportion to their size.

Protection

132. **Clothing.** Wear two thicknesses of light clothing: mosquitos bite through one layer but rarely through two. Tuck your trouser legs in your boots and your sleeves in your gloves. Whenever you can, cover bare flesh with clothing.

133. **Headnets.** Make sure your headnet is well tucked in to the collar of the shirt.

134. **Insect Repellant.** Apply to the face and exposed skin every four hours. Apply to the face even when wearing a headnet; midges are small enough to penetrate the mesh.

135. **Smudge Fires.** Any green wood or green leaves will produce an insect repelling smoke.

136. **Parachute Canopies.** In summer, the aircraft may be used as a shelter and can be made insect-proof with parachute canopies.

TRAVEL

137. The experience of Arctic crashes reveals that the best policy for survivors is to stay with the crashed aircraft and await rescue. Travel to a camp site should be undertaken, however, if the scene of the crash is endangered by natural hazards, such as crevasses and avalanches. There may be times when walking home is considered to be the only solution.

Considerations

138. **Your Position.** Have you been able to fix your position? Quite often the reason for crash landing is that the aircraft is lost. An approximate position, say within 50 miles, is worthwhile for the purpose of narrowing the search by air. But it is not accurate enough to use as a departure point in an attempt to walk out. You must know the exact location of your camp and your objective.

139. **Wireless Contact.** Is the search organization aware of your plight and your position? Was your distress message acknowledged? Have you made wireless contact since the crash?

140. **Physical Condition.** Even with snow shoes and skis, Arctic travel is slow, strenuous, and hazardous. Don't overestimate your physical capabilities.

141. **Weather.** The weather should be assessed from two angles. Is the prevailing weather likely to hinder search forces? Is the weather conducive to an Arctic route-march and sleep in temporary shelters?

142. **Orientation.** You must have reliable methods of determining and maintaining your intended route. In the barren lands particularly, you must have a compass. Should you lose your compass the following methods may be used to determine direction:—

(a) *Sky Map.* A high uniform overcast reflects the surrounding terrain. Clouds over open water, timber, or snow-free ground will appear black, while clouds over sea ice or uniform snow covering will appear white. Pack ice or drifted snow are indicated by a mottled appearance on the surface of the cloud. New ice is indicated by greyish patches on the sky map. A careful study of the earth's reflection on the clouds may be used for determining the proper direction to travel.

(b) *Bird Habits.* Migrating waterfowl fly towards the land in the thaw. Most sea birds fly out to sea in the morning and return to land at night.

(c) *Vegetation.* Although there are few trees on the tundra, the moss theory still applies; moss is heaviest on the north side. The bark of the alders is lighter in colour on the south side than on the north side. Don't rely on one observation; make several and average the direction. Lichens on rocks are most numerous on the south side, where they receive the greatest warmth of the sun.

(*d*) **Stars.** In the northern hemisphere, true north can be ascertained from the constellation of the Great Bear, which points to Polaris (North Star), the star over the North Pole. Trying to estimate your latitude by measuring the angle of Polaris above the horizon will give you only a very approximate result, unless you have a sextant and tables. In the southern hemisphere, the Southern Cross indicates the direction of south. Other constellations, such as Orion, rise in the east and set in the west, moving to the south of you when you are north of the equator and vice versa.

(*e*) **Sun.** If you have the correct local time on your watch, the shadow cast by an object at 1200 hours will indicate north and south. The object must be perpendicular to the ground and straight. In the northern hemisphere the base of the shadow will indicate south and the tip will indicate north. If you have no watch, place a straight object in the ground or snow on a level spot. Starting in the morning, and continuing about once every hour throughout the day, mark the point at the tip of the shadow. At the end of the day, connect these points and you will have a line which runs true east and west. The shortest distance between the base of the shadow and the east-west line will indicate north and south. The method of determining direction by pointing the hour hand of a watch at the sun is considered inaccurate and should not be used.

143. **Final Decision.** A crashed aircraft with a prominent signals area is more likely to be spotted from the air than a man on the march with limited signalling devices. Your final decision should be based on two factors: your nearness to civilization and the probability of rescue. Once you have made your decision, stick to it. This decision will have been reached after considering all the factors when your minds were fresh. As time goes on, your powers of reasoning will deteriorate and there may be a tendency to consider the factors individually instead of collectively. However, if it is at all possible, or if you are in any doubt, *stay with the aircraft.*

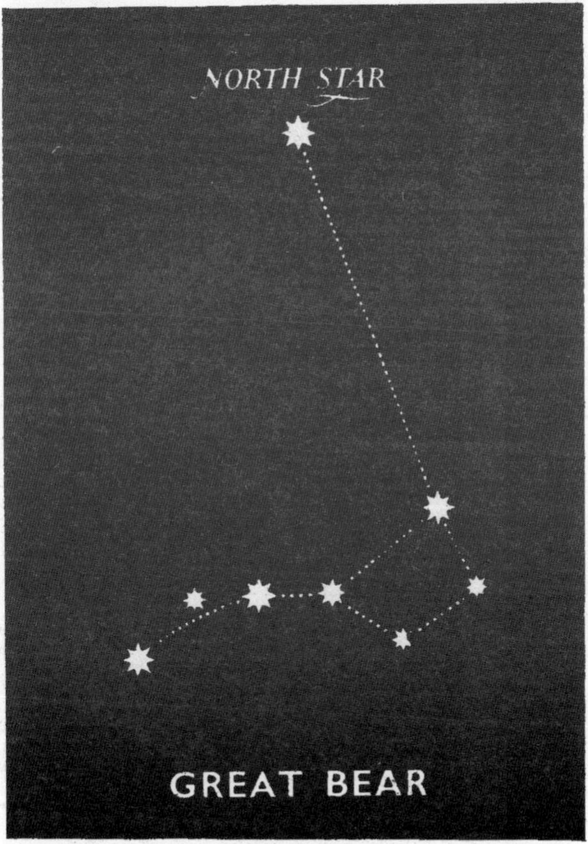

Fig. 42. Great Bear and North Star

SOUTHERN CROSS

FALSE CROSS

S

SOUTHERN CROSS

Fig. 43. Southern Cross

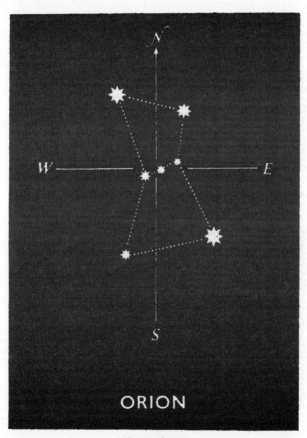

Fig. 44. Orion

Routes

144. The majority of the settlements are to be found on the rivers or on the coast. Water is the highway of the north. Dog teams and sledge trains travel on the ice in the winter. In addition, food and fuel are available along the waterways both in summer and winter. Travel downstream to reach civilization, except in Siberia where the rivers flow north.

145. **Mountain Routes.** Mountain routes, where ice caps, glaciers, crevasses, and avalanches may be encountered, are extremely hazardous and should be used only if there is no alternative. The minimum requirements are a climbing rope, two ice axes, and an experienced leader. If any one of these is not available select another route. In areas where avalanches are prevalent, travel in the early morning when it is coldest. At all times proceed with extreme caution.

146. **Timber Country.** Snow lies deep in timber country and travel is extremely difficult without snowshoes or skis. Two miles a day in these circumstances is good progress. Trail breaking is very strenuous, and it should be taken in turns for periods of not more than five minutes. Rest for five minutes about every half-an-hour. When possible travel by the rivers. Make a raft or use your dinghy in the summer, and travel on foot over the ice in winter. When travelling on river ice keep on the inside of the bends; the swifter current on the outside of the bends wears the ice away from below. At river junctions walk on the far side, or take to the land until you are well downstream from the junction. When river travel is not feasible, travel along ridges. In winter the snow does not lie deep on the ridges; in summer the ridges are drier and firmer under foot.

147. **Barren Land Routes.** Barren land travel without snowshoes or skis is difficult and slow. You cannot afford to follow the rivers, which wind and twist and greatly increase the distance to be covered. Beware of thin ice on the edges of tundra lakes and in the connecting channels. Lack of landmarks, blowing snow, and fog, emphasize the need of a compass for barren land travel. If your tracks are clear, check your course by taking back bearings of your tracks; otherwise proceed in single file about 30 paces

apart. The last man carries the compass and, using the middle men as sighting objects, controls the course of the first man by calling out instructions to him. Constant compass checks will ensure that you are travelling in a straight line, which is the shortest distance. Summer travel in the barren lands presents another problem. Soggy vegetation and bogs make the going slippery and heavy. Tundra lakes, quicksands, and swamps must be avoided. In these circumstances it is usually preferable to float down a river than to travel across country.

148. **Sea Ice Routes.** On sea ice travel in one party; there is nothing to be gained by anyone who remains behind. The problems of coursekeeping are identical with those on the barren lands, but the movement of ice floes makes it difficult to determine your actual track. Pressure ridges and hummocks may be used as landmarks over short distances only, since they are constantly moving. The unreliability of the magnetic compass in high latitudes necessitates course checks on the sun and stars. Avoid tall, pinnacled icebergs which are liable to capsize. For shelter at sea, look for low, flat-topped icebergs.

149. **Trail Equipment.** The amount of equipment you can take on the trail will depend on what you can carry, or haul on improvised sledges. Individual packs, adapted from the personal survival packs, should be worn high up on the shoulders and should not exceed a weight of 35 pounds. Avoid carrying whenever possible; float down the rivers in summer and haul a sledge in winter. Sledges can be made from cowlings, doors, pieces of fuselage, or timber. A single tow line attached to a bridle, with individual shoulder loops tied in, is preferable for travel over snow. Only one trail need necessarily be broken. Over ice, it is better to have several towlines attached to the bridle, since they enable each man to choose his own footholds. It may be necessary to leave behind many useful articles. Basically you will require food, shelter, and fuel, or means of obtaining them. The value of each piece of equipment must be carefully considered. For instance, a fuel stove is superfluous in timber country, but is an absolute necessity on sea ice. Always carry spare clothes and a sleeping bag. Travel is difficult over any terrain without snowshoes or skis. Short wide skis are best; they should be about three

feet long and eight inches wide. They can be made of metal or timber. Snowshoes, which are simply load-spreaders, can be made of metal tubing, spruce, or willow. Finer limbs can be woven in and secured with shroud lines.

150. **Preparation.** While the advice to all survivors is *"Stay with the aircraft"*, the possibility of the necessity for travel should be recognized at the beginning of the survival period. Items of equipment such as snowshoes, skis, and sledges, should be made and tested before setting out on the trail. Indeed, they will be very useful around the camp site for collecting fuel and foraging for food.

151. **Blaze your Trail.** If the entire survival party is going to walk out, or if a small group is setting out to get help, messages stating the intended route should be left at the base camp. In the Arctic communication is very slow, and the more signs of your presence left along the trail the greater is your chance of being found. Mark your trail clearly. Strange trails are nearly always

Fig. 45. Trail Blazing

followed by trappers and Eskimos. On the trail make your camp well before nightfall; leave plenty of time to build your shelter, prepare emergency signals, and have a hot meal. The following morning, all signals, particularly snow writing, should be changed to large arrows showing the direction the party has taken.

152. Finally, it must again be strongly emphasized that if you are in any doubt at all **stay with the aircraft.**

E43541 Wt.38194-BN.3823 5,700 7/53 Gp.8 Fosh & Cross Ltd., London

Notes

Notes

....
....
....
....
....
....
....
....
....
....
....
....
....
....
....
....
....
....
....
....

Notes

....
....
....
....
....
....
....
....
....
....
....
....
....
....
....
....
....
....
....

Notes

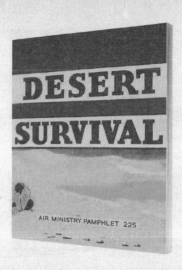

First issued to airmen in the 1950s, this reprint of The Air Ministry's Desert Survival pamphlet includes emergency advice to crew operating over desert regions.

Packed with original line drawings and instruction in:

- How to find water in a dry stream course
- How to make a hat out of seat cushions

OUT NOW

First issued to airmen in the 1950s, this reprint of The Air Ministry's Sea Survival pamphlet includes emergency advice to crew operating over sea regions.

Packed with original line drawings and instruction in:

- How to punch man-eating sharks, which are 'cowards'

- The pros and cons of drinking 'fish juice'

- When to smoke

OUT NOW

First issued to airmen in the 1950s, this reprint of The Air Ministry's Jungle Survival pamphlet includes emergency advice to crew operating over jungle regions.

Packed with original line drawings and instruction in:

- What to do if 'jungle hiking becomes boring'

- How to stay safe from poisonous reptiles and insects

- The benefits of using a 'fire thong'

OUT NOW